Let's visit a
FRUIT FARM

Sarah Doughty
and
Diana Bentley
Reading Consultant
University of Reading

Photographs by
Paul Seheult

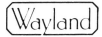

Let's Visit a Farm

Beef Farm
Cereal Farm
Dairy Farm
Fish Farm
Fruit Farm
Market Garden
Pig Farm
Poultry Farm
Sheep Farm

First published in 1989 by
Wayland (Publishers) Ltd
61 Western Road, Hove
East Sussex, BN3 1JD, England

British Library Cataloguing in Publication Data
Doughty, Sarah
    Let's visit a fruit farm.
    1. Fruit. Cultivation
    I. Title   II. Bentley, Diana
    III. Seheult, Paul IV. Series
    634

ISBN 1–85210–750–2

Phototypeset by
Kalligraphics Ltd
Horley, Surrey
Printed and bound by
Casterman S.A.,Belgium

Contents

This is the fruit farm in Kent 8

Here is the fruit farmer and his family 11

In winter young apple trees are planted in
    the ground 12

The older trees are pruned in winter 14

In spring the bees pollinate the flowers 16

In summer the apples begin to grow 18

Tree-training and spraying takes place in
    summer 20

In autumn the apples are picked from the trees 22

The apples are washed and stored 24

The apples are sorted and packed into boxes 26

Glossary 28

Books to read 29

Index 30

All the words that appear in
bold are explained in the
glossary on page 28.

This is the fruit farm in Kent

Farmhouse

Packhouse

Cold storage sheds

The farm

Old barn

Cold storage shed

Apple orchards

9

Here is the fruit farmer and his family

Here are Mr and Mrs Mount with their children. The children are called Camilla and Sam. Mr Mount is a fruit farmer. In his **orchards** he grows apple trees.

There is plenty of work for the farmer to do on a fruit farm, so Mr Mount has people to help him. Here he is talking to one of the farm workers.

In winter young apple trees are planted in the ground

In winter, a fruit farmer buys young fruit trees from a **nursery.** The farm workers carry the trees on a trailer to the orchard. They plant the trees in rows. A tree's stem is weak so it is tied to a **stake.** This gives the tree support as it grows. In two years time, the trees will be big enough to produce apples.

13

The older trees are pruned in winter

These apple trees are older and produce apples every autumn. In the winter the farm workers prune the trees. This means that some of the branches and twigs are cut off using a saw or **secateurs.** This stops the tree from growing too big. It also helps the tree to grow a healthy crop of fruit the next year.

In spring the bees pollinate the flowers

In May all the apple trees have pink blossom. The flowers need to be **pollinated** by bees to grow fruit. A bee-keeper comes to the farm with **hives** of bees. He wears a special suit to protect himself from the bees when he opens the hives.

The farmer wants the bees to carry **pollen** from flower to flower. This helps the plants to make their seeds. These seeds will later grow into fruits.

In summer the apples begin to grow

In the summer the apples begin to grow. The tiny fruits are called fruitlets. The farmer wants them to grow into big, healthy fruits. So farm workers pick some of the unwanted fruitlets off the tree by hand. This is called thinning. It means that the farmer will grow a smaller crop of better fruit. The apples that are left on the tree can now grow bigger and tastier.

19

Tree-training and spraying takes place in summer

Tree-training in summer helps apple trees to grow the right shape. The tree's branches are tied down to its stem or a stake using a length of string. This keeps the tree tidy.

This tractor is carrying a sprayer. It sprays the trees to prevent pests and diseases damaging the fruit.

In autumn the apples are picked from the trees

In autumn the apples are picked off the trees. This is called the harvest. As the trees are quite small it is easy for most people to reach the higher branches. The apples are put into apple picking buckets. When they are full, the apples are emptied into big bulk bins.

The apples are washed and stored

With a large crop of fruit only some of the apples can be sold at once. The rest have to go into cold storage sheds. First, the apples go through a machine called a **deluger.** This washes the fruit and prepares them for storage. Then the crates of apples are stacked up inside the storage sheds. Some of the apples stay here for up to six months before they are sold to the shops.

The apples are sorted and packed into boxes

Before the apples are sold they go to the farm's packhouse. Here the apples are sorted by hand into different classes. This means the better apples are separated from the others. The apples are then sorted by machine into different sizes. The apples are finally packed into boxes ready to go to the local shops and supermarkets.

Look out for British apples the next time you go to the fruit shop – they will have come from a fruit farm very much like Mr Mount's.

27

Glossary

Deluger A machine that washes crates of apples by spraying them with water.

Hives Places where bees live together.

Nursery A place where young trees and plants are grown.

Orchard Land where fruit trees are grown.

Pollen A powder that is produced by one part of a flower to make another part develop seeds.

Pollinated When pollen has been passed from one part of a flower to another.

Secateurs A small pair of shears.

Stake A wooden stick that has been driven into the ground.

Acknowledgement

The publishers would like to thank the farmer and his staff for their help and co-operation in the making of this book.

Books to read

Fruit by Stephanie W. Craven (Ladybird, 1979)
Fruit by Jacqueline Dineen (Young Library, 1987)
Fruit Salad – A First look at Fruit by Julia Eccleshare
   (Hamilton, 1986)
Apple Trees by Sylvia A. Johnson (Lerner, 1984)
Apple Tree by Barrie Watts (A & C Black, 1986)

Places to visit

Notes for parents and teachers

To find out more about visiting a fruit farm, or any other type of farm in your area, you might like to get in touch with the following organizations:

The Association of Agriculture (Farm Visits Service), Victoria Chambers, 16-20 Strutton Ground, London SW1P 2HP.
They have produced a useful booklet called *Farms to Visit in Britain* which gives details of farms that are open to the public, many with special facilities for schools.

The National Union of Farmers, Agriculture House, 25-31 Knightsbridge, London SW1X 7NJ.
Local branches organize visits to farms. Their addresses can be obtained from your library.

County Colleges of Agriculture
These exist in most counties. Many have an established Schools Liaison or Environmental Studies Unit. Contact the Association of Agriculture if you have difficulty in locating your local College of Agriculture.

Index

apples 11, 12, 14,
    18, 22, 23, 24,
    26

bees 16, 17
blossom 17

deluger 24

farmer 11
fruitlets 18

harvest 23

nursery 12

orchard 11, 12

packhouse 26
picking 22
planting 12
pollination 16, 17
pruning 14

shops 26
spraying 20, 21
storage 24

thinning 18
trees 11, 12, 14, 17,
    18, 20, 21, 22, 23
tree-training 20, 21